THE STRUCTURED METHOD OF PEDAGOGY

*Effective Teaching in the Era of the New Mission
for Public Education in the United States*

Emile V. Tabea, Ed.D.

THE STRUCTURED METHOD OF PEDAGOGY
EFFECTIVE TEACHING IN THE ERA OF THE NEW MISSION
FOR PUBLIC EDUCATION IN THE UNITED STATES

iUniverse books may be ordered through booksellers or by contacting:

iUniverse
1663 Liberty Drive
Bloomington, IN 47403
www.iuniverse.com
1-800-Authors (1-800-288-4677)

Because of the dynamic nature of the Internet, any web addresses or links contained in this book may have changed since publication and may no longer be valid. The views expressed in this work are solely those of the author and do not necessarily reflect the views of the publisher, and the publisher hereby disclaims any responsibility for them.

Any people depicted in stock imagery provided by Getty Images are models, and such images are being used for illustrative purposes only.
Certain stock imagery © Getty Images.

ISBN: 978-1-5320-6489-0 (sc)
ISBN: 978-1-5320-6490-6 (e)

Print information available on the last page.

iUniverse rev. date: 12/15/2018

THE STRUCTURED METHOD OF PEDAGOGY

Effective Teaching in the Era of the New Mission
for Public Education in the United States

Emile V. Tabea, Ed.D.

THE STRUCTURED METHOD OF PEDAGOGY
EFFECTIVE TEACHING IN THE ERA OF THE NEW MISSION
FOR PUBLIC EDUCATION IN THE UNITED STATES

iUniverse books may be ordered through booksellers or by contacting:

iUniverse
1663 Liberty Drive
Bloomington, IN 47403
www.iuniverse.com
1-800-Authors (1-800-288-4677)

Because of the dynamic nature of the Internet, any web addresses or links contained in this book may have changed since publication and may no longer be valid. The views expressed in this work are solely those of the author and do not necessarily reflect the views of the publisher, and the publisher hereby disclaims any responsibility for them.

Any people depicted in stock imagery provided by Getty Images are models, and such images are being used for illustrative purposes only.
Certain stock imagery © Getty Images.

ISBN: 978-1-5320-6489-0 (sc)
ISBN: 978-1-5320-6490-6 (e)

Print information available on the last page.

iUniverse rev. date: 12/15/2018

For my wife Melanie and my children Joel and Eunice, who always encourage me to do anything I set my mind to, as long as that anything is educational. Thank you guys, for your love for education, peace and harmony among humans!

CONTENTS

INTRODUCTION

I am sure classroom teachers or anyone who has tried teaching will agree with me that teaching is not an easy task. The many steps involved in the teaching process make the task difficult, steps such as knowing one's students, developing lesson objectives, teaching to the objectives, assessing student learning, re-teaching to the objectives if necessary and more. One thought went into this guide: to improve education by way of helping teachers of all grades to become effective in the classroom. Whether you are an educator at the elementary, middle or high school level, a University professor, or planning to be a teacher, regardless of the subject you are teaching or are preparing to teach, you are challenged to serve as a key instrument in student achievement and therefore an instrument in the improvement of education. Learning, compared to acquisition, lasts a lifetime. With increased technology and rapid change, learning is imperative just to "keep up" with the 21st century and the new skills that come with it.

CHAPTER 1

The Structured Method of Pedagogy: A Brief Presentation

The structured method of pedagogy is a research-based and validated instructional method that has proven effective in addressing the academic needs of students in the United States including students whose first language is not English. This method referred to as "sheltered instruction," was developed in a national research project sponsored by the Center for Research on Education, Diversity and Excellence (CREDE) (from 1996 to 2003), a national research center funded by the U.S. Department of Education. The goal of the project was to assist the population of students in U.S. schools, including those at risk of educational failure, to achieve academic excellence. The authors of the project are Jana Echevarria and Mary Ellen Vogt, researchers at the California state University, Long Beach, and Deborah J. Short, of the Washington-based Center for Applied Linguistics. With the collaboration of practicing teachers, these researchers reviewed the literature on the best teaching practices and identified what education consultant, writer and public speaker William Lezotte (1997) called *high-yield instructional strategies*.

Lezotte (1997) defines *high-yield strategy* as a "concept or principle supported by research or case literature that will, when successfully applied in a real school setting, result in significant improvement in assessed student achievement" (p. 18).

The Structured Method of Pedagogy and its High-Yield *Instructional* Strategies:

The structured method of pedagogy consists of eight interrelated high-yield instructional strategies. The eight strategies as identified by Echevarria, Vogt and Short (2008) are as follows:

1. Writing of well-defined content objectives for your lesson

2. Building of background knowledge

3. Providing comprehensible input

4. Teaching of strategies to learn and retain information

5. Giving students opportunities to interact in the classroom

6. Creation of application activities that extend learning

7. Monitoring of lessons to determine if delivery is supporting the objectives

8. Review of lessons and frequent assessment of students' progress

The chapters that follow provide a detailed description of the eight high-yield instructional strategies as presented above.

CHAPTER 2

High-Yield Instructional Strategy

Number One:

Write well-defined content and language objectives for your lesson

The first of the eight high-yield instructional strategies associated with the structured method of pedagogy is the writing of well-defined content objectives for your lesson, or lesson preparation (Echevarria, Vogt & Short, 2008).

▪ Write no more than two well-defined content objectives for the lesson you want to teach, display these objectives in class for review with students, so that they are all aware of what it is that you (the teacher) want them to know and be able to do at the end of your lesson

As a teacher, it is good practice to write down well-defined instructional objectives for the lesson you want to teach, what it is that you want your students to know and accomplish at the end of your lesson.

Mager (1962) defines an *objective* as "an intent communicated by a statement describing a proposed change in a learner—a statement of what the learner is to be like when he has successfully completed a learning experience. It is a description of a pattern of behavior (performance) we want the learner to be able to demonstrate (p.3).

You will be called a good teacher and always be remembered as one if you know what you want for your students and take each of them from the basic level of thinking to the next level.

When you were a student, if someone were to ask you to try to remember *one* teacher who you felt had the most influence on your life and to write down the characteristics of that teacher as well as you can remember them, chances are that among the characteristics of your favorite teacher was the fact that that teacher

- knew you as an individual

- knew what he or she wanted for you

- (probably) had a significant influence on your life, as he

- played a part in the development of your attitudes, the formation of your habits, and the acquisition of information that was new and exciting to you

- may have guided you subtly or may have directly "pushed" you towards these behavior changes

- may have used a great many visual aids or none at all, or may have given multiple-choice tests, essay tests, or no test at all.

This is to say that what effective teachers have in common is not their teaching styles or techniques, or the kinds of tests they use. Rather, it is **what** they accomplish, **not how** they accomplish it that matters. The lesson here is that if you the teacher, want to make a difference in the lives of your students, *you must know what you want your students to accomplish* at the end of your lesson.

After you have written well-defined instructional objectives for the lesson you want to teach, the structured method of pedagogy requires that you the teacher **display in class** those instructional objectives for **review** with your students prior to beginning instruction. The purpose for the display and review of instructional objectives, as TenBrink (1999) indicates, is to adequately prepare students for an instructional event and will help them to get the most out of it (Cooper, 1999).

Criteria of a well-defined content objective

As TenBrink (1999) explains, to be said "well-defined," a content objective must be

1. Student oriented
2. Descriptive of a learning outcome
3. Clear and understandable, and
4. Observable

1. Student-oriented content objectives

A content objective that is student-oriented places an emphasis on student behavior, not on teacher behavior; it places an emphasis on what students are expected to do, not on what the teacher will do.

Examples of student-oriented content objectives

1. Students should be able to write down their observations of a simple experiment, stating what was done and what happened.

2. Students should be able to list the five punctuation rules discussed in the textbook.

3. When given the description of a form of government, students should be able to classify that form of government and list its probable strengths and weaknesses.

Activity

Read the following objectives and write *"S"* before the student-oriented objectives and *"T"* before the teacher-oriented objectives.

_____ **1.** To help the students appreciate classical music.

_____ **2.** To maintain discipline in my class.

_____ **3.** To carry out an investigation using the scientific method.

_____ **4.** To write a unified paragraph on a single topic.

_____ **5.** To read at least 250 words per minute with no less than 80 percent comprehension.

_____ **6.** To outline my lecture on the board before class begins.

Now let's review your answers for correctness. If you misidentified more than three objectives, you may want to reread this section before you go on.

■■■

2. Content objective descriptive of a learning outcome

A content objective that is descriptive of a learning outcome describes the learning outcome, not the learning activities that lead to that outcome. It is sequentially-appropriate; that is, it is appropriate for the developmental level of students, making sure that prerequisite skills are attained before starting to work on a new objective.

3. Clear and understandable content objectives

A well-defined content objective is explicit, unambiguous, uses verbs that leave less room for interpretation. In other words, when writing content objectives, you must use verbs that describe a definite action or behavior, verbs that have only one meaning, not two or more meanings.

Examples of clear and understandable content objectives

1. The students should be able to use a yardstick to measure the length, width, and height of any of piece of furniture in the room. The measurements should be accurate to within half an inch.

2. The students should be able to identify correctly the ingredients in a mixture of chemicals prepared in advance by the teacher.

3. When given a contemporary poem, the students should be able to evaluate it according to the criteria discussed in class.

Activity

For each of the following objectives, determine whether it has a single meaning, two or more meanings by marking **1, 2 or 3** in the space provided.

_____ **1.** The student should be able to label the parts of the heart correctly on a diagram of the heart similar to the one on page 58 of the text.

_____ **2.** The student should be able to list in writing the presidents of the United States.

_____ **3.** The students should be able to know the presidents of the United States.

_____ **4.** The students should be able to recognize and call by name each president of the United States on seeing his picture.

_____ **5.** The students should be able to appreciate music.

Now let's review your answers for correctness. If you misidentified more than three objectives, you may want to reread this section before going on.

■■

4. Observable content objectives

A well-defined content objective is observable; that is it has an **explicit verb** and (usually) a **well-defined object of the verb.** These two requirements help make an objective clear and unambiguous. A third requirement for an observable objective is that the verb must **describe an observable action,** an action that results in an observable product.

Examples of observable objectives

1. When given words from the list in the back of the spelling book, the students should be able to _identify_ (explicit verb) words that are _incorrectly spelled_ (object) and make any necessary corrections.

2. Given several occasions to listen to different types of music, the students will _select_ at least _three different types_ of music he or she likes.

3. The students should be able to _list_ the _major parts of a friendly letter,_ briefly _describing_ the _function of each part._

4. The students should be able to _identify_ correctly the _ingredients in a mixture of chemicals prepared in advance_ by the teacher.

The following verbs are to be avoided when writing content objectives as they are vague and unobservable:

to know   to value

to understand   to cope with

to appreciate	to like
to grasp	to love
to comprehend	to familiarize
to believe	to realize
to think	to enjoy

The verbs that follow describe observable actions or actions that yield observable products. When you write instructional objectives, use these kinds of verbs:

to identify	to choose	to select
to speak	to compute	to draw
to list	to add	to infer
to isolate	to separate	to locate
to explain	to predict	to solve
to divide	to analyze	to investigate

OBSERVATION WORKSHEET
Review and Analysis of Objectives

This activity is designed to give you the opportunity to examine instructional objectives, identifying their strengths and weaknesses according to the criteria set forth in this chapter.

Directions: Do not use actual names of schools, teachers, administrators, or students when using this worksheet.

Observer's Name: _____

Date: _____

Grade Level: _____

Subject: _____

Class Size: _____

Source of Objectives (lesson plans; course syllabus; teacher's manual): _____

Background Information: Give a brief description of the school's social, economic, and ethnic makeup.

_____
_____
_____

What to Record: Ask the teacher you are observing for copies of the instructional objectives he/she is using to guide his/her teaching for the day or week. These objectives may be part of the teacher's lesson plans, the course syllabus, or in the teacher's manual.

Reflection on your Observation: Summarize your findings, indicating the major strengths and weaknesses of the instructional objectives you reviewed. For each objective, determine whether or not it meets the following criteria:

1. Well-defined? (Yes/NO): Explain _____

2. Student-oriented? (Yes/NO): Explain _____

3. Sequentially appropriate? (Yes/NO): Explain _____

4. Developmentally appropriate? (Yes/NO): Explain _____

5. Describe a learning outcome? (Yes/NO): Explain _____

6. Clear, unambiguous? (Yes/NO): Explain _____

7. Observable? (Yes/NO): Explain _____

8. Attainable by the students within a reasonable time limit? (Yes/NO): Explain _____

9. In harmony with the overall goal of the course (and curriculum)? (Yes/NO): Explain _____

10. In harmony with the overall goals and values of the institution? (Yes/NO): Explain _____

Source: (TenBrink, D. T. in Cooper, J., 1999)

Writing and displaying language objectives for your lesson

There is a second pedagogical task associated with the lesson preparation strategy and that is the writing and displaying of no more than two language objectives for your lesson.

In the same way you wrote and displayed well-defined content objectives for your lesson, the lesson preparation strategy requires that you the teacher

■**Clearly define no more than two language objectives for your lesson, display these objectives in class for review with your students, so that they are all aware of what they should know and be able to do at the end of your lesson**

What this means is that when planning your lesson, after you have written no more than two well-defined content objectives, you must also write no more than two well-defined language objectives, incorporate in your lesson activities that support students' language development. As Echevarria, Vogt & Short (2008) point out, students need activities that will develop their receptive language capabilities (listening and reading skills) as well as their productive language capabilities (speaking and writing).

Characteristics of well-defined language objectives

To avoid repetition, I must inform that the criteria for writing well-defined language objectives are the same as the criteria for writing content objectives; that is, the language objectives that you will write for your lesson must be:

1. Student-oriented
2. Descriptive of an appropriate learning outcome
3. Clear and understandable, and
4. Observable

Examples of verbs used for writing language objectives:

define	find the main idea	rehearse
retell	compare	persuade
listen for	summarize	write

Table 3.11: Features of objective definition and display component

Self-Assessment: Review the contents of the table below and mark the box that most closely represents your current pedagogical practices:

D = Daily, O = Occasionally, N = Never.

Content and language definition and display component of the structured	D	O	N
1. I write and display cleary-defined content objectives			
2. I write and display cleary-defined language objectives			
3. I use district curriculum guidelines and grade-level content standards as guides to select the concepts I wish to teach			
4. I use grade-level supplementary materials (models, visuals computer programs…etc.) to make the lesson clear			
5. I give students meaningful activities (surveys, letter writing, simulations… etc.) that integrate lesson concepts with language practice opportunities for reading, writing, listening and/or speaking			

CHAPTER 3

High-Yield Instructional Strategy

Number Two:

Build Students' Background Knowledge

Background knowledge building is the second of the *eight high-yield instructional strategies* associated with the structured method of pedagogy (Echevarria, Vogt & Short, 2008).

As a teacher, you must know that effective teaching takes students from where they are and leads them to a higher level of understanding (Vygotsky, 1978; Krashen, 1985). Suppose you are teaching a carefully prepared lesson with which your students cannot connect; you are explaining new concepts and you observe some confused faces, off-task behaviors, and some mumbling among students. While there may be several reasons why your students don't understand your lesson, one common reason is a mismatch between what your students have learned and experienced in the past and the concepts that you are teaching. To help students understand your lesson, you must build their background knowledge. What this means is that you must take a few minutes to find out what your students know or have experienced about the topic you want to teach. After you have identified what your students know about your topic, you must engage in the following three tasks:

▪ **Link explicitly concepts to students' background experiences**

All students have prior knowledge, gained from school and life experiences. You the teacher can informally assess what students know and can do, so that you can help them connect what they know with what you are teaching. You can help your students make appropriate connections if your explanations are more concrete with supplementary materials such as photos, models, illustrations, videos related to the topic you are teaching.

▪ Link explicitly past learning to new concepts

For learning to occur, new information must be integrated with what students have previously learned. You must build a bridge between previous lessons and concepts and the lesson you are teaching. You must explicitly point out how past learning is related to the information at hand. You can do this by reviewing key information in prior lessons, discussion questions such as

"Who remembers what we learned about_____? How does that relate to our chapter?" You can also link past learning to new information at hand by reviewing class notes, PowerPoint slides related to the topic at hand

▪ Teach key vocabulary in the content area text

Academic language or vocabulary development is strongly related to academic achievement. You must teach key vocabulary as a pre-reading step to increase your students' comprehension and achievement. Academic language is the vocabulary and language used in the classroom.

Academic language has three key elements:

Content words: These are vocabulary words, terms, and concepts associated with a particular topic being taught

Process/Function Words: These are words that have to do with functional language (i.e. how to justify opinions, state a conclusion, language used in the classroom for processes and tasks

Words and word parts that teach language structure: Words based on the morphology of the language of instruction

Examples of Questions that Build Students' Background Knowledge:

-What does…….mean to you?

-What do you already know about………. Why?

-What are your thoughts about………… Why?

-Have you ever seen a……..?

-Does this remind you of other things we have learned about?

-What would it feel like to be.........?

Table 2.10: Features of Background Knowledge Building Strategy

Self-Assessment: Review the contents of the table below and mark the box that most closely represents your current pedagogical practices:

D = Daily, O = Occasionally, N = Never.

Teaching practices that build background knowledge	D	O	N
1. I link concepts explicitly to students' background experiences			
2. I explicitly make links between students' past learning and new concepts			
3. I emphasize key vocabulary words (e.g. highlight new vocabulary words, write them down on the board for students to see, review new words with students)			

CHAPTER 4

High-Yield Instructional Strategy

Number Three:

Provide Comprehensible Input

Have you ever taught a lesson that students did not get? If so, this may be because you did not provide comprehensible input. Unless you can make what you are teaching understandable, you are wasting your time.

Comprehensible input consists of:

- Using vocabulary that students can understand

- Explaining academic tasks clearly

- Using a variety of techniques (modeling, hands-on activities, gestures, visuals, film clips) to make content concepts clear

Table 3.10: Features of Comprehensible Input Strategy

Self-Assessment: Review the contents of the table below and mark the box that most closely represents your current pedagogical practices:

D = Daily, O = Occasionally, N = Never.

Teaching practices that provide comprehensible input	D	O	N
1. I use speech appropriate for students' proficiency level (e.g., slower speech rate, enunciation, and simple sentence understandable to all students)			
2. I explain clearly academic tasks to students			
3. I use a variety of techniques to make content concepts clear (e.g. modeling, use of visuals, hands-on activities, demonstrations, gestures, body language)			

CHAPTER 5

High-Yield Instructional Strategy

Number Four:

Teach learning strategies

Now that we have discussed elements of effective planning, background building, and comprehensible input, let us now discuss ways we can facilitate student learning. You can teach your students learning strategies they can use to facilitate the learning of the materials you have planned to teach. Learning strategies are defined as "special thoughts or behaviors that individuals use to help them comprehend, learn, or retain information (O'Malley & Chamot, 1990, p.1). They are about ways we can help students connect what they know to what they are learning. To be an effective teacher, you must teach your students techniques and methods for learning and retaining information, give them ample opportunities to use learning strategies, review and assess the strategies with them. When students are taught learning strategies, they can become autonomous, control, direct, expand and improve their own learning.

There are three types of learning strategies you can teach students (O'Malley & Chamot, 1990).

1) **Metacognitive Strategies.** This is the process of purposefully monitoring one's own thinking. Metacognitive Strategies help students monitor their own comprehension through self-questioning and taking corrective action if understanding fails.

2) **Cognitive Strategies.** These are strategies that help students organize the information they are expected to learn. They are used by learners when they mentally and/or physically manipulate material, or when they apply a specific technique to a learning task (Bake & Brown, 1984).

    Examples of cognitive strategies that learners use to enhance their own understanding are

    a) Previewing a story prior to reading

    b) Establishing a purpose for reading

    c) Consciously making connections between personal experiences and what is happening in a story

d) Taking notes during a lecture

e) Completing a graphic organizer

f) Creating a semantic map (McLaughlin & Allen, 2002).

The third and last type of learning strategy you can teach students is

3) **Social/Affective Strategies.** These are student-centered strategies whereby students participate in a group discussion or cooperative learning to solve a problem.

Teaching a variety of learning strategies is not enough (Lipson & Wixson, 2008). Rather, learners also need to know the following:

1) What a strategy is **(declarative knowledge)**

2) How to use the strategy they learned **(procedural knowledge)** and

3) When to use a given strategy and explain why they use the strategy they learned **(conditional knowledge)**

You can use CALLA (the **C**ognitive **A**cademic **L**anguage **L**earning **A**pproach) to promote student learning. CALLA is an instructional model for teaching both content and language and that incorporates student development of metacognitive, cognitive and socioaffective strategies that students can apply in instructional tasks. CALLA helps students to do the following:

1. Develop their capacity to monitor their own thinking **(metacognition)**

2. Organize the information they are expected to learn **(cognitive strategy)**

3. Participate in cooperative learning groups to solve problems **(socioaffective strategy)**

You can teach students content with expository texts by having them use the following six steps strategy:

Survey the text: You can have students preview and scan the text to be read for about one minute to determine key the concepts that will be learned.

Generate questions: You can have students generate questions in groups, questions likely to be answered by reading the text. You the teacher will post student questions on chart paper and mark with multiple asterisks those questions that are frequently suggested by the groups.

Make predictions: Ask the whole class to come up with three to four key concepts they THINK they will learn while reading; ask students to base their predictions on the previously generated questions, especially those you will mark with asterisks.

Read the text and search for answers: In pairs or small groups, ask students to read the text and search for answers to their generated questions and confirm or disconfirm their predictions; use sticky notes to mark answers to questions and spots where predictions have been confirmed

Respond to questions: Have students answer questions (not necessarily in writing) with partners or group members; have them formulate new questions for the next section of text to be read (if the text is lengthy); you the teacher will lead discussion of key concepts, clarifying any misunderstandings

Summarize key concepts: Have students summarize the text's key concepts (orally or in writing) using key vocabulary where appropriate

All of the above requirements are based on the following facts:

1. Mentally active learners are better learners
2. Learning strategies can be taught
3. Learning strategies are transferable to new tasks
4. Academic language learning is more effective with learning strategies

▪ Use scaffolding techniques consistently to assist and support students' understanding

Scaffolding is a term associated with Lev Vygotsky's (1978) Zone of Proximal Development or ZPD. The ZPD is the difference between what a student can accomplish alone and what he or she can accomplish with the assistance of the teacher or a more experienced individual. You can scaffold instruction by providing substantial amounts of support and assistance in the earliest stages of teaching of a new concept or strategy, and by decreasing gradually the amount of support as students acquire experience through multiple practice opportunities (Vacca, 2002).

You can use two types of scaffolding techniques to assist and support student understanding, *verbal scaffolding* and *procedural scaffolding*. Verbal scaffolding consists of the use of prompting, questioning, and elaboration to facilitate students' movement from lower levels of language proficiency, comprehension and thinking to higher levels of language proficiency, comprehension, and thinking.

Examples of verbal scaffolding are:

1) Paraphrasing, that is restating a student's response in order to model correct language usage.
2) Using "think-alouds.
3) Reinforcing contextual definitions—an example of this is "most Ivorians, the natives of Cote D' Ivoire prefer to pursue their education in Europe." The phrase "the natives of Cote D' Ivoire" provide a definition of the word "Ivorians" within the context of the sentence.
4) Providing correct pronunciations by repeating students' responses
5) Slowing down the rate of speech, pausing between phrases, and allowing students the wait time they may need to process information.

The second type of scaffolding techniques you (the teacher) can use to assist and support student understanding is *procedural scaffolding*.

Procedural scaffolding consists of:

1) Explicit teaching, modeling, practice opportunities with other students, and expectations for independent application
2) One-on-one-teaching, coaching, and modeling
3) Small group instruction with children practicing a newly learned strategy with another more experienced student
4) Partnering students with more experienced readers assisting those with less experience (Nagel, 2001).

You can also use Bloom's taxonomy (1956) of educational objectives, which will be discussed later in this book, to ask students questions that promote critical thinking. As a teacher you can use Bloom's taxonomy of educational objectives **as learning proceeds from concrete knowledge to abstract values,** or from denotative to connotative knowledge.

Teach students how to determine levels of questions, and teach them also to ask their own questions at varying levels of Bloom's levels of taxonomy. This will help students develop hypotheses using the scientific method. Teaching students to ask their own questions will help them to develop the research skills they MUST learn and practice before completing their education program.

Table 4.10: Features of Learning Strategy Component

Self-Assessment: Using the table below, mark the box that most closely represents your current pedagogical practices:

D = Daily, O = Occasionally, N = Never.

	D	O	N
1. I provide ample opportunities for students to use learning strategies			
2. I use scaffolding techniques (e.g., think aloud) to assist student understanding			
3. I use a variety of questions or tasks that promote higher-order thinking skills (e.g., literal, analytical, and interpretive questions)			

CHAPTER 6

High-Yield Instructional Strategy

Number Five:

Provide activities that promote student interaction

In order to be an effective teacher, you must interact with your students frequently and have your students interact among themselves frequently. Interaction need not always be oral. You can interact with students through **dialogue journals**, sharing ideas and learning, and modeling appropriate written text. In secondary classes, you can have students **partner with one another**. Students can also interact using technology or through a pen pal e-mail exchange with another class elsewhere in the world. You must allow sufficient time for student to clarify key concepts or responses during interactions.

FIGURE 5.10: Pedagogical practices that promote interaction

Self-Assessment: Using the table below, mark the box that most closely represents your current pedagogical practices:

D = Daily, O = Occasionally, N = Never.

	D	O	N
1. I provide opportunities for frequent student interaction and discussion			
2. I move from whole group to cooperative groups or partners to support language and content objectives of the lesson, increase student involvement in the learning process			
3. I consistently allow sufficient wait time for student responses			
4. I provide ample opportunities for students to clarify key concepts in their first language (L1) as needed with aide, peers, or L1 text (if any)			

CHAPTER 7

High-Yield Instructional Strategy

Number Six:

Give students application activities that extend learning

Up to this point, we have discussed the following:

1) Writing content and language objectives for the lesson you want to teach
2) Activating student prior knowledge of the subject you are about to teach and introducing key vocabulary
3) Selecting a learning strategy and higher-order questions for students to focus on
4) Developing a scaffolding approach for teaching the new information
5) Planning for student interaction

The practice and application component is about giving your students a chance to practice with the new material and with your careful oversight. You the teacher must give your students a chance to demonstrate how well they are learning the material you are teaching. Practice helps students master a skill (Jensen, 2005; Marzano, Pickering, & Pollock, 2001). Make sure the practice and application tasks you will develop aim for practice of all four language skills:

a) Reading
b) Writing
c) Listening
d) Speaking

The practice and application component requires that you

a) Supply lots of hands-on materials
b) Provide activities for students to apply content/language knowledge as discussing and doing make abstract concepts concrete

c) Allow students to work in partnership with other students before working alone

d) Integrate all language skills (speaking, listening, reading and writing) into each lesson

FIGURE 6.10: Features of Practice/Application Component

Self-Assessment: Using the pedagogical tasks below, mark the box that most closely represents your current teaching practices:

D = Daily, O = Occasionally, N = Never.

	D	O	N
1. I provide hands-on materials and/or manipulatives for students to practice using new content knowledge			
2. I provide activities for students to apply content and language knowledge in the classroom			
3. I provide activities that integrate all language skills (i.e., reading writing, listening, and speaking			

CHAPTER 8

High-Yield Instructional Strategy

Number Seven:

Monitor your lesson

The structured method of pedagogy requires that you the teacher

1. Monitor your lessons to determine if the delivery is supporting the language and content objectives
2. List strategies for improving student time-on-task throughout the lesson
3. Generate activities to keep students engaged ninety-to hundred-percent (90% to 100%) of the class period
4. Evaluate a situation whereby a great lesson plan is not delivered successfully and explain what might have gone wrong and what could be improved

Lesson preparation and lesson delivery are closely related.

To have students engaged does not mean that students have to be highly active; that they have to be writing, reading and moving the entire time. This simply means to have all students follow the lesson, think and speak, respond to your direction approximately ninety to hundred percent (90% to 100%) of the period. To engage students in your lesson, you can have the whole class think of an answer to a question, give students time to think or reflect every ten minutes. In other words, use classroom time effectively by minimizing off-tasks behaviors such as passing out and handling papers, and making announcements. As a teacher, your students will learn if you are explicit in your expectations and make certain that they know which materials they will be assessed on.

FIGURE 7.10: Features of Lesson Delivery Component

Self-Assessment: Using the pedagogical tasks below, mark the box that most closely represents your current teaching practices:

D = Daily, O = Occasionally, N = Never.

	D	O	N
1. I monitor my lesson to determine if the delivery is supporting the objectives			
2. I have strategies to improve students' time-on-task throughout the lesson			
3. I generate activities to keep students engaged ninety-to hundred-percent (90% to 100%) of the class period			
4. I evaluate situations whereby a great lesson plan is not delivered successfully and explain what might have gone wrong and what could be improved			

CHAPTER 9

High-Yield Instructional Strategy Number

Number Eight:

Review your lesson and assess students' progress

The structured method of pedagogy requires that you frequently assess students' progress and use the results of your findings to plan your lesson. You can be called an effective teacher if you use findings of student assessment to plan your lesson. There are two reasons to assess student learning. One is to use the results of student assessment to plan your lessons according to students' needs and strengths, and the other is to evaluate how effectively your lessons have been delivered. As a teacher you must assess student learning of your lesson's content and language objectives throughout the lesson. As a teacher, you want to make sure your students understand what you are trying to teach them.

Assessment and Evaluation

There is a distinction between assessment and evaluation (Lipson & Wixson, 2008). To *assess* is to gather and synthesize information about students' learning. To *evaluate* is to "make judgment about students' learning. The two processes can be viewed as progressive: first assessment; then, evaluation" (McLaughlin, & Vogt, 1996, pp. 104, 106). You must assess students' learning in periodic reviews to determine if they understand and are applying content concepts.

You MUST link assessment to instruction and assessment needs to target the lesson objectives. In the same way students need to know what the lesson objectives are, they need to be informed about how and what types of assessment they will have.

Toward the end of the lesson that you are trying to teach, assess your students' progress to see whether it is necessary to review and reteach the lesson. This type of assessment is informal, authentic, multidimensional, and includes multiple indicators that reflect student learning, achievement, and attitudes.

An informal assessment involves ongoing opportunities for determining the extent to which students are learning the content you are trying to teach. It includes tasks that occur within regular instruction and that are not intended to be graded or evaluated according to set criteria. Examples of informal assessments are

- Observations

- Anecdotal reports

- Teacher-to-student conversations

- Student-to-student conversations

- Quick-writes, and

- Brainstorming

An authentic assessment is assessment in which you the teacher engage students in meaningful tasks that take place in real-life contexts. Authentic assessment is usually *multidimensional* in that different ways are used to determine whether students have met the content or language objective, or progressing toward meeting the lesson objectives. The different ways you can use in an authentic assessment are written pieces, audiotapes, student and parent interviews, videotapes, observations, creative work and art, discussion, performance, oral group responses.

FIGURE 8.10: Features of Review/Assessment Component

Self-Assessment: Using the features below, mark the box that most closely represents your current teaching practices:

D = Daily, O = Occasionally, N = Never.

Self-Assessment: Using the features below, mark the box that most closely represents your current teaching practices:

D = Daily, O = Occasionally, N = Never.

	D	O	N
1. I review key vocabulary words			
2. I review key content concepts			

3. I provide feedback regularly to student on their ouput (e.g., language, content, work)			
4. I assess students' comprehension and learning of all lesson objectives (e.g., spot checking, group response, group response) throughout the lesson			

CHAPTER 10
Bloom's Taxonomy of Educational Objectives

Background Information

Dr. Benjamin Bloom is the most talked about educator in U.S. schools and colleges today, for his tremendous contribution to the field of education. In 1956, this American educator, in collaboration with his colleagues Max Englehart, Edward Furst, Walter Hill, and David Krathwohl published a framework for categorizing educational objectives or thinking skills. This framework came to be known as *Bloom's Taxonomy*, which has been applied by generations of K-12 teachers as well as professors as a planning tool.

The idea behind the taxonomy is that what educators want students to know can be organized into levels of thinking skills, from the most basic level of thinking to the more complex. The levels of thinking skills as classified by Bloom et al. (1956) are successive, so that one level of thinking can be mastered before the next level can be reached.

Bloom's taxonomy of educational objectives

The taxonomy as published by Bloom et al. (1956) is nothing but a classification system of educational objectives or thinking skills, which Bloom organized into six levels. From the most basic level to the more complex, the six levels of thinking skills as identified by Bloom are as follows:

1. The knowledge (memorization or recall) level

2. The comprehension (or understanding) level

3. The application level

4. The analysis level

5. The synthesis level (or creation) and

6. The evaluation level

(see tables 1 and 2 on next page, original and revised taxonomy)

Evaluation

Synthesis

Analysis

Application

Comprehension

Knowledge

Table 1 (Top): Original Taxonomy of Educational Objectives
Source: Learning to think, thinking to learn, p. 8, Pohl, 2000.

Evaluate

Create

Analyze

Apply

Understand

Remember

Source: Bloom's taxonomy revised (Anderson & Krathwohl, 2001).

As it can be seen in the second table, Anderson and Krathwohl (2001) revised Bloom's taxonomy and changed the original levels **from nouns to active verbs** to fit the more outcome-focused modern education objectives. The authors also reversed the order of the highest two levels of learning objectives.

Below is a presentation of Bloom's taxonomy and what assessment questions at each of the levels require of students:

Level 1: Knowledge and Memory

Knowledge is the first level in Bloom's classification system of learning objectives.

When you ask students questions at the knowledge level of the taxonomy, you are simply asking them to recognize or recall information, ideas, and principles in the approximate form in which they were learned. You are NOT asking them to manipulate information, but simply to remember it just as it was learned, to remember facts, observations, and definitions that have been learned previously.

Examples of verbs used for writing knowledge level objectives:

define	read	recite	name
recall	count	identify	reproduce
recognize	indicate	trace	repeat
remember	list	review	relate
point	name	write	record
draw	record	state	select

Examples of knowledge level assessment questions

What happened after…?	Can you name…?
Who was it that…?	Who spoke to…?
How many…?	Find the meaning of…
What is…?	Describe what happened after…
Which is true or false…?	

Some drawbacks to knowledge level assessment questions

Knowledge level questions

- Rely only on memory, ask students to "spit back" the information they have memorized from their text and class notes
- Assess only a superficial and shallow understanding of an area
- Do not ask students to demonstrate real understanding
- Tend to be overused by teachers

Some benefits of knowledge level questions

Knowledge level questions

- Promote classroom participation and high success experiences for both low-ability and high-ability students
- Provide low-ability and high-ability students with high success opportunities
- Are necessary steps on the way to more complex, higher-order questions; Yes, you the teacher cannot ask students to think at higher levels if they lack fundamental information

■■

Level 2: Comprehension

Comprehension is the second level in Bloom's classification system of learning objectives. When you give your students comprehension-level questions to answer, you are asking them to

- Demonstrate sufficient understanding to organize and arrange material mentally
- Go beyond recall of information and select those facts that are pertinent to answer questions
- Demonstrate a personal grasp of material by being able to rephrase it, give a personal description of material in their own words, or
- Use the material to make comparisons
- Interpret and translate material that is presented on charts, graphs, tables, and cartoons

Examples of verbs used for writing comprehension level objectives:

| describe | discuss | estimate |
| compare | restate | report |

contrast	explain	review
differentiate	distinguish	translate
compute	predict	extrapolate

Examples of comprehension level assessment questions

What was the main idea…?

Can you clarify…?

Can you illustrate…?

Does everyone act in the way that………..does?

Can you write in your own words?

How would you explain…?

Can you write a brief outline…?

Who do you think…?

What do you think could happen next…?

■■

Level 3: Application

Application is the third level in Bloom's classification system of learning objectives. When you give your students application-level questions to work on, you are asking them to

- Go beyond memorization and interpretation of what they have memorized
- Apply previously learned information to reach an answer to a problem
- Apply a rule or process to a problem to determine the single right answer to that problem

Examples of verbs used for writing application level objectives:

| Demonstrate | locate | solve | employ |
| examine | order | use | restate |

illustrate	predict	utilize
interpret	illustrate	translate
operate	relate	report

Examples of application level assessment questions

Which factors would you change if…?

What questions would you ask of…?

Do you know of another instance where…?

From the information given, can you develop a set of instructions about…?

In each of the following cases, which of Newton's laws is being demonstrated?

According to our definition of socialism, which of the following nations would be considered socialist today and why?

■■

Level 4: Analysis

Analysis is the fourth level in Bloom's classification system of learning objectives. When you give your students analysis level questions to work on, you are asking them to

- Think critically and in depth
- Take time to think and analyze
- Identify motives, reasons, uncover evidence, and reach conclusions
- Identify causes for a specific occurrence
- Consider and analyze available information to reach a conclusion, infer or generalize based on this information

Examples of verbs used for writing analysis level objectives:

| Justify | categorize/dissect | analyze |
| deduce | compare/contrast | support |

investigate	detect	determine evidence
summarize	distinguish	draw conclusion
identify motives or causes	experiment	
debate	criticize	infer
inspect	criticize	separate

Examples of analysis level assessment questions

What are some of the problems of …?

Can you distinguish between…?

What were some of the motives behind…?

What was the turning point?

What was the problem with…?

How is … similar to?

What do you see as possible outcomes?

Which events could not have happened?

If… happened, what might the ending have been?

1. Analysis questions ask students to analyze information to support a particular conclusion, make inferences or generalizations based on evidence, available information

What evidence can you cite to validate that smoking cigarettes is more harmful than drinking alcohol?

How does role-play promote cultural understanding?

Which of the speaker's points support affirmative action?

2. Analysis questions ask students to draw a conclusion, make inferences or generalization based on evidence, available information

After studying major developments in South Africa and China, what can you now conclude about the various causes of revolutionary change?

After reading this story, how would you characterize the author's background, attitude, and point of view?

Look at this new invention. What do you think the purpose of this invention is?

3. **Analysis questions ask students to identify the causes or reasons for certain events through analysis**

Why did the congresswoman decide not to run for the presidency?

What factors influence the writing of the author?

How do your personal finances respond to economic upswings and downturns?

■■

Level 5: Synthesis

Synthesis is the fifth level in Bloom's classification system of learning objectives. When you give your students synthesis level questions, you are asking them to

- Be creative
- Produce or perform original and creative communications
- Make predictions, allowing a variety of creative answers
- Solve problems, allowing a variety of creative answers

Examples of verbs used for writing synthesis level objectives:

design	predict	imagine
develop	construct	create
produce	how can we improve…?	invent
Synthesize	what would happen if…?	estimate
Write	how can we solve…?	combine
Estimate	hypothesize	

Examples of synthesis level assessment questions

How many ways can you...?

Can you create new and unusual uses for...?

Can you develop a proposal which would...?

What would happen if...?

What don't you devise your own way to...?

Can you see a possible solution to...?

Can you design a...to...?

1. Synthesis questions ask students to make predictions

What would the United States be like if the South had won the Civil War?

How would your life be different if school were not mandatory?

After studying about forestry on the West Coast, what do you suspect is happening in the South American rain forests?

2. Synthesis questions ask students to solve problems

How can we successfully raise money to fund our homeless shelter project?

How would you measure the height of a building without being able to go into it?

Design a musical instrument (with materials found in our lab) that effectively demonstrates three principles of physics

3. Synthesis questions ask students to produce original communications

Write an e-mail to a local newspaper editor on a social issue of concern to you

What would be a descriptive and exciting name for this video game?

Construct a collage of pictures that represents your values and feelings

■■

Level 6: Evaluation

Evaluation is the last level of Bloom's *Taxonomy* of learning objectives. Like the synthesis and analysis levels, evaluation is a higher-order mental process as questions at this level do not necessarily have a single correct answer.

When you give your students evaluation level questions, you are asking them to

- Judge the merit of an idea, a solution to a problem, or an aesthetic work
- Offer an opinion on an issue

Examples of verbs used for writing evaluation level objectives:

assess	conclude	critique
evaluate	verify	review
argue	rate	rank
decide	select	determine
judge	recommend	measure
estimate	choose	
score		

Examples of evaluation level assessment questions

Do you think…is a good or bad thing?

How would you have handled…?

What changes to…would you recommend?

Do you believe…? How would you feel if…?

What are the consequences of…?

What are the pros and cons of...?

Why is... of value?

Do you think...is good or bad things?

Can you defend your position about...?

Who will gain and who will lose?

Give three reasons why this picture is your best

How do you assess your performance at school?

Decide why young children should or should not be allowed to read any book they want

----

OBSERVATION WORKSHEET
Focus on Higher Order Questions

Given the rapid pace of classroom dialog, capturing the level of a teacher's questions can be challenging. Here is an approach that will help you analyze a teacher's use (or nonuse) of higher-order questions.

Directions: Do not use actual names of schools, teachers, administrators, or students when using this worksheet.

Observer's Name: _____

Date: _____

Grade Level taught: _____

Subject: _____

Class Size: _____

Background Information: Give a brief description of the school's social, economic, and ethnic makeup.

_____

_____

_____

What to Record: Write down each question asked in class for later analysis. After the observation, assess each question in terms of Bloom's Taxonomy to determine which of the six cognitive levels most appropriately describes the cognitive demand of each question. Some questions may be related to class procedures or other nonacademic areas, so you may want to create a seventh category called "Other" for these non-instructional questions.

Reflections on your Observation:

1. How are the teacher's questions distributed across Bloom's taxonomy?

_____

_____

_____

2. Are some levels underutilized or not used at all? Are some categories overused?

3. Although no one has defined an "ideal" distribution, as a result of this observation, what are some factors that you think are important in using the different levels of the taxonomy?

■■

Functions of well-defined objectives

Now that you can state the criteria for well-defined content objectives and know how to write them, I will discuss the usefulness of instructional objectives and where they can be found.

Instructional objectives can help you

1. Focus your planning

- Decide, out of the material to be covered, what you really want your students to know or be able to do
- Eliminate topics that are of lesser importance and highlight the more important subject matter

- Determine if your plans include a balance of memorization, conceptualization, problem solving, and so forth
- Determine if you have planned for sufficient higher-order learning outcomes

Well-defined instructional objectives can help you do the following:

2. Plan effective instructional events

- Design instructional events that will produce the expected learning outcome

For example,

Memorization of information: If an instructional objective calls for the students to memorize information, the instructional events or activities should be designed to get students to repeat that information, to form appropriate associations to attain the instructional objective.

Learning of a new concept: If an instructional objective calls for the students to learn a new concept, the instructional events should be designed to get students to focus on the critical attributes of the concepts to be learned, and to compare and contrast positive and negative instances

By instructional event I mean an instructional activity or set of activities in which students are engaged (with or without the teacher) for the purpose of learning, attaining an instructional objective

Examples of instructional events: Listening to a teacher's explanation, watching a film, doing an assignment in history, and completing a workbook page.

To plan appropriate instructional events, first, you must determine the kind of learning involved in each instructional objective. To do this should be relatively easy if your instructional objectives are well defined. **The secret is in the verbs.** The verbs should signal the kind of learning involved in instructional objectives. For example,

Verbs that suggest memory learning: *recall, list, describe*

Verbs that suggest discrimination learning: *distinguish, differentiate, contrast*

Verbs that suggest concept learning: *categorize, identify, recognize*

Verbs that suggest problem solving: *diagnose, solve, resolve, determine*

Verbs that suggest affective learning: desire, enjoy, like, prefer

Verbs that suggest skill learning: *manipulate, perform, do, physically control*

After you have determined the kind of learning called for by an objective, your next step is to determine the kind of activities that the students have to do to accomplish that kind of learning. After determining the kind of learning involved in each instructional objective, everything you do must be designed to help the students do what they need to do to learn. You must, not only help provide the students with the information they need, but you must also help them process that information in appropriate ways. Asking students the right kinds of questions at the right time helps them to process new information.

Well-defined instructional objectives can help you

3. Plan valid evaluation procedures

When evaluating learning, you must make sure that the test designed to evaluate student learning is valid. A test is valid if it measures what it is supposed to measure, and that is each of the instructional objectives taught in the classroom. Because instructional objectives define the expected learning outcomes, they are the key to developing valid tests.

The third task of the lesson preparation component of the SIOP model of pedagogy requires that you

▪ Carefully choose the content concepts you wish to teach

When planning lessons around content concepts, make sure you take into consideration students' first language literacy, their second language proficiency, their reading ability, the cultural and age appropriateness of the materials, and the difficulty of the material to be learned (Echevarria, Vogt & Short, 2008).

The fourth task of the lesson preparation component requires that you

▪ Use many supplemental materials that support the core curriculum and contextualize learning

It is a good practice to plan for supplementary materials that will enhance meaning and clarify confusing concepts. Supplementary materials provide a real life context and enable students to bridge prior experiences with new learning. By using a variety of materials, you can support different learning styles and multiple intelligences. Because information and concepts are presented in a multifaceted manner, students can see, hear, feel, perform, create, and participate in order to make connections and construct personal, relevant meanings. Examples of supplementary materials include the following:

Real-life objects

Hands-on manipulative objects

Pictures

Visuals

Multimedia

Demonstrations

Related literature

Adapted text

The fifth task of the lesson preparation component requires that you

- **Adapt content to all levels of student proficiency**

You must find ways to make difficult texts and other resource materials accessible for all students, leaving content concepts intact. Some of the instructional strategies you can use are prereading, during reading, postreading, graphic organizers, and outlines.

The sixth and last task of the lesson preparation component requires that you

- **Provide your students with meaningful and authentic activities that integrate lesson concepts with language practice opportunities**

Your students will learn if you can help them relate classroom experiences to their own lives. Make sure classroom experiences mirror that which actually occurs in your students' world.

Table 1.10: Features of Lesson Preparation Component

Self-Assessment: Using the features below, mark the box that most closely represents your current teaching practices:

D = Daily, O = Occasionally, N = Never.

	D	O	N
1. I define clearly content objectives for students			
2. I define clearly language objectives for students			
3. I make sure content concepts are appropriate for age and educational background level of students			
4. I use supplementary materials to a high degree to make the lesson clear and meaningful (i. e. graphs, models, visuals)			
5. I make sure content (e.g. text, assignment) is adapted to all levels of student proficiency			
6. I develop meaningful activities that integrate lesson concepts (e.g. interviews, letter writing, simulations, models) with language practice opportunities for reading, writing, listening, and/or speaking			

CHAPTER 11
Gardner's Theory of Multiple Intelligences (MI)

As a teacher, for all your students to learn, you must assess and gather facts about how each one of them learns best— their learning preferences, modes, styles or strengths and differentiate instruction based on their learning styles. In other words, more students will learn if you support the different modes of learning in your classrooms.

Cognitive psychologist Howard Gardner's theory of multiple intelligences (MI) is based on the belief that we all have strengths, weaknesses and unique combinations of abilities; we all have multiple intelligences—capacities to solve problems within us to varying degree. And if you the teacher know each of your students' strengths and support those strengths, your students will learn. As Gardner (1983) explains, it is very unusual for someone to be strong in one intelligence and extremely weak in the other, maybe because intelligences interact with one another (*Frames of mind & Multiple Intelligences: The Theory in Practice, 1983*).

Gardner (1983) identified eight categories of intelligences within all people. The eight intelligences within each one of us as identified by Gardner and a description of capabilities are discussed below.

As you assess each of your students' intelligences, check items that apply to each of your students.

Intelligence 1:

Linguistic Intelligence

A student who has linguistic intelligence

_____ writes better than average for age

_____ spins tall tales or tells jokes and stories

_____ has a good memory for names, places, dates, or trivia

_____ enjoys word games

_____ enjoys reading books

_____ spells words accurately (or if prescribed, does developmental spelling

_____ that is advanced for age)

_____ appreciates nonsense rhymes, puns, tongue twisters

_____ enjoys listening to the spoken word (stories, commentary on the radio, talking books)

_____ has a good vocabulary for age

_____ communicates to others in a highly verbal way.

Intelligence 2:

Logical-Mathematical Intelligence

A student who has logical-Mathematical intelligence

_____ asks a lot of questions about how things work

_____ enjoys working or playing with numbers

_____ enjoys math class (or if preschool, enjoys counting and doing other things with numbers)

_____ finds math and computer games interesting (or if no exposure to computers, enjoys other math or science games)

_____ enjoys playing chess, checkers, or other strategy games

_____ enjoys working on logic puzzles or brainteasers (or if preschool, enjoys hearing logical nonsense)

_____ enjoys putting things in categories, hierarchies, or other logical patterns

_____ likes to do experiments in science-related subjects.

Intelligence 3:

Spatial Intelligence

A student who has spatial intelligence

_____ reports clear visual images

_____ reads maps, charts, and diagrams more easily than text (or if preschool, enjoys looking at more than text)

_____ daydreams a lot

_____ enjoys art activities

_____ is good at drawings

_____ likes to view movies, slides, other visual presentations

_____ enjoys doing puzzles, mazes, or visual activities

_____ builds interesting three-dimensional constructions (e.g. LEGO buildings)

_____ gets more out of pictures than words while reading

_____ doodles on workbooks, worksheets, or other materials.

Intelligence 4:

Bodily-Kinesthetic Intelligence

A student who has bodily-kinesthetic intelligence

_____ has a dramatic way of expressing himself/herself

_____ enjoys running, jumping, wrestling, or similar activities (or if older, will show these interests in a more "restrained" way—e.g., running to class, jumping over a chair)

_____ shows skill in a craft (e.g. woodworking, sewing, mechanics) or good fine-motor coordination in other ways

_____ excels in one or more sports (or if preschool, shows physical activities advanced for age)

_____ loves to take things apart and put them back together again

_____ puts his/her hands all over something he/she has just seen

_____ cleverly mimics other people's gestures or mannerisms.

Intelligence 5:

Musical Intelligence

A student who has musical intelligence

_____ has a good singing voice

_____ plays a musical instrument or sings in a choir or other group

_____ has a rhythmic way of speaking and/or moving

_____ unconsciously hums to himself/herself

_____ taps rhythmically on the table or desk as he/she works

_____ responds favorably when a piece of music is put on

_____ remembers melodies of songs

_____ can tell you when music sounds off-key or disturbing in some other way.

Intelligence 6:

Interpersonal Intelligence

A student who has interpersonal intelligence

_____ has two or more close friends

_____ enjoys socializing with peers

_____ gives advice to friends who have problems

_____ seems to be a natural leader

_____ likes to play games with other kids

_____ is sought out by peers for socialization

_____ has a good sense of empathy or concern for others

_____ enjoys informally teaching other kids

_____ belongs to clubs, committees, organizations, or informal peer grouping

_____ seems to be street-smart.

Intelligence 7:

Interpersonal Intelligence

A student who has intrapersonal intelligence

_____ prefers working alone to working with others

_____ has a good sense of self-direction

_____ does well when left alone to play or study

_____ has a realistic sense of his/her abilities and weaknesses

_____ displays a sense of independence or a strong will

_____ has good self-esteem

_____ is able to learn from his/her failures and successes in life

_____ accurately expresses how he/she is feeling

_____ has an interest or hobby that he/she does not talk about much

_____ marches to the beat of a different drummer in his/her style of living and learning.

Intelligence 8:

Naturalist Intelligence

A student who has naturalist intelligence

_____ enjoys doing nature projects, such as bird watching, butterfly or insect collections, tree study, or raising animals

_____ speaks out in class for the rights of animals, or the preservation of planet earth

_____ does well in topics at school that involve living systems (e.g., biological topics in science, environmental issues in social studies)

_____ brings to school bugs, flowers, leaves, or other natural things to share with classmates or teachers

_____ gets excited when studying about ecology, nature, plants, or animals

_____ likes to water and tend to the plants in the classroom

_____ likes field trips in nature, to the zoo, or to natural history museum

_____ talks a lot about favorite pets, or preferred spots in nature, during class sharing.

CONCLUSION

The structured method of pedagogy has eight pedagogical components and thirty pedagogical tasks: The lesson preparation component with six teaching tasks; the background building component with three teaching tasks; the comprehensible input component with three teaching tasks; the interaction component with four teaching tasks; the practice and application component with three teaching tasks; the lesson delivery component with four tasks; last but not least, the review and assessment component with three teaching tasks.

All the pedagogical components described in this guide (with the exception of the preparation component) do not have to be implemented in the hierarchy or order in which they are discussed here. They can be presented in any order as they are interrelated or integrated into lessons. For example, as you begin to write structured-based lesson plans, you will see that the tasks involved in comprehensible input are necessary from the beginning to the end of a lesson, and students must interact throughout your lesson in order to master its language objectives. As a teacher, if you decide to implement all the components of the structured method of pedagogy as presented in this book, this is just fine. What is important is the presence of all eight pedagogical components and the thirty tasks in your lessons.

REFERENCES

Anderson, L. W. & Krathwohl, D.R. (eds). (2001). A taxonomy of learning, teaching and assessing: A revision of Boom's taxonomy of educational objectives: Longman.
Baker, L., & Brown, A. L. (1984). Metacognitive skills and reading. In P. D. Pearson, R. Barr, Kamil M.L. and Mosenthal P. (Eds.), Handbook of Reading Research (pp. 353-394). New York: Longman.

Bloom, B. (1956). Taxonomy of educational objectives Handbook II: Affective domain (The classification of educational goals). Philadelphia, PA. David McKay Publications.

Chamot, A. U., & O'Malley, J. M. (1994). The CALLA handbook: How to implement the Cognitive Academic Language Learning Approach Reading, MA: Addison-Wesley.

Cooper, D. J. (1999). Literacy: Helping children construct meaning. 4th Ed. Boston, MA: Houghtin Mifflin.

Echevarria, J., Short, D. & Vogt, M. (2008). Making content comprehensible for English language learners : The SIOP model. 3rd Ed. Boston, MA: Pearson/Allyn & Bacon.

Echevarria, J., Vogt, M., Short, D. (2004). Making content comprehensible for English

Learners: The SIOP Model (2nd Edition). Boston: Allyn & Bacon.

Gardner, H. (1983). Frames of mind and Multiple Intelligences: the theory in practice: New York: Basic Books.

James, C.(1999). Classroom teaching skills, 6th Ed. Boston, MA. Houghton Mifflin Company.

Jensen, E. (2005). Teaching with the brain in mind. Alexandria, VA: ASCD.

Krashen, S. (1985). Literacy before schooling. London, England. Heinemann.

Krashen, S. (1985). The input hypothesis: issues and implications. London: Longman.

Lezotte, W. (1997). Learning for all: Whatever it takes. Mebberville, MI. Effective schools products.

Mager, R. F. (1962). Preparing instructional objectives. Belmont, CA: Fearon Publishers. Inc.

Marzano, R. J., Pickering, D., & Pollock, J. E. (2001). Classroom instruction that works: Research-based strategies for increasing student achievement. Alexandria, VA: ASCD.

McLaughlin, M. & Allen, M. B. (2002). Guided comprehension: A teaching model for grades 3-8. Newark, DE: International Reading Association.

O'Malley, J.M. & A.U. Chamot. (1990). Learning strategies in Second Language Acquisition. Cambridge: Cambridge University Press.

Pohl, Michael. (2000). Learning to Think, Thinking to Learn: Models and Strategies to Develop a Classroom Culture of Thinking. Cheltenham, Vic.: Hawker Brownlow.

Vacca, R. T. (2002). Content area reading: Literacy and learning across the curriculum, 7th Edition. Boston, MA. Pearson Education.

Vygotsky, L. (1962). Thought and language. Cambridge, MA. Harvard University Press.

Vygotsky, L. (1978). Mind in society: The development of higher psychological processes. Cambridge, MA. Harvard University Press.